Crying, Through GOD'S Eyes

KEITH M. KING

Keith M. King

This book is an original idea written by Keith M. King. No parts of this book shall be duplicated, reproduced, or shared without the writer's permission. By reading this book, you are agreeing to such terms.

Crying, Through GOD's Eyes Copyright © 2014 by Keith M. King.

All rights reserved.

Written and created by Keith M. King

Editor: Jill Duska with Devoe Publications www.kdevoe.com

Typesetting and Interior design: Devoe Publications www.kdevoe.com

Cover Design: Donna Osborne Clark with Devoe Publications www.kdevoe.com

ISBN-13: 978-0-692-32256-7

ISBN-10: 0692322566

Crying Through GOD's Eyes

Ad feedback

Customer Reviews

3
5.0 out of 5 stars

5 star	100%
4 star	0%
3 star	0%
2 star	0%
1 star	0%

Top Customer Reviews

By Jo'ntel Johnson on December 27, 2016
Format: Paperback
This book has blessed me tremendously, I love it. If anyone is looking for a book filled with understanding on how to receive blessings from God, well this is the book. I recommend that you purchase this book.

By essie on January 26, 2015
Format: Kindle Edition
I truly enjoyed reading this book. It was written from the Bible. I am looking forward to his next book.

By EBONY on December 15, 2016
Format: Paperback
THIS BOOK TOUCHED MY HEART AND SOUL.

Keith M. King

Books Written By Author:

Keith M. King

Crying, Through GOD'S Eyes

The Power of my Words!

The Open Doors of Success

The Open Doors of Success
Volume II

Sow your seed of determination and you will reap restoration in the end.

This book is dedicated to each and every person that lives and wants to accept Jesus Christ as their Lord and Savior.

Since 1992 I seriously want to get God's word out to everyone that I come in contact with. I was baptized in the Holy Ghost on April 27, 1992 around 6:00p.m. which was on a Tuesday evening. Since then I have received a calling on my life, and that calling is to try to save as many souls as I can. I have up until now only used word of mouth to inform the individuals that I meet and also to the ones that I already know about getting God's word out to them. I am not an ordained minister; at least not yet, therefore I do not have the use of the pulpit as a way of communication. Needless to say, I have been limited on getting the word out to people other than the ones that I see every day.

This year I came up with the idea of writing a book as a way of communicating to the public on just how awesome our Heavenly Father is. Also how He made it so easy for us to be prosperous. I never in my wildest dreams thought that I could write a book. I started out by just putting words down on paper, using expressions of what the Holy Ghost gave me to say, and giving scriptures that I receive from the Holy Spirit that will help others. As I kept writing more and more started to come to

Enlightenment

Being nineteen years old with a calling from God is a good thing for a young man with his whole life in front of him. The fact of the matter is not just having a calling, but not knowing that God had chosen him for a great mission in life. This young man entered into the military at the age of eighteen. Somehow he always felt there was something different about him. Wanting to fit in with the majority; he did some of the things the average young man his age would do.

Even though the young man was young in age, he was very well sophisticated. Having been throughout many different states any times and now many different countries while in the service at such a young age is something not many young men his age could brag about. I was enlightened by this young man that he was very well happy, but there was still something missing in his life.

At the age of nineteen I saw a drastic change in the young lad, some of the things that he use to do he didn't want to do anymore. He explained that he was uncomfortable with doing certain things. The young lad informed me that he was filled with this great compassion for his fellow man and all of God's beautiful creation.

He knew there was a purpose for everything, a reason God created everything in its form, everything relies on everything. The great mystery had just been solved; the entire creation relies on the entire creation to exist. Not one of God's creations can survive by itself. The tree needs water, the water needs the cloud to carry it to the tree, and the tree needs the bird to carry its seed through its dropping throughout the land to create more trees.

As I studied this young man I found him to be very wise in many areas of his life. I also found out that he makes mistakes, sometime dumb decisions; but as I studied him I found out that if he would take time to ponder over a decision and not rush into it he would always make the right choices. This is where I saw the hand of God leading and guiding him in the direction to prosper through this life.

If I could call it for what it is, I would say that God was helping this lad to renew his mind at a young age. This is what renewing your mind is, it's about letting the Father lead you as you totally depend on him.

As I conclude, renewing your mind is not a bad experience; it will lead you to a place in your life that will be far better than it would be if you were to think in the same way before you did renew your mind. Before I end I just want to let you the reader know that the young man that I was speaking of is me. God has blessed me tremendously throughout my life, and he is still blessing me in ways that you can't imagine. God is a good God; always have been and always will be.

I pray that you will take time out to read this book and apply it to your life and watch how my God will turn your life around and put a smile on your face that will light up any room that you walk into.

Acknowledgments

"To God be the Glory"

It is to my wonderful mother Evangelist Mary L. King and my dad the late Mr. Alfred King that I give honor to for bringing me up in a wonderful Christian home. I thank God for my parents; one thing I can say I never saw them drunk, fighting, or even using abusive profane language towards me or my siblings or anyone else. These are the type of parents not everyone is blessed to have. I am truly grateful.

Now to my siblings Claudette, Lynn, Arnold, Joseph, Antonia, and even (Deborah) who is deceased. Thank you too; without your knowing it you also played a special part in my life. As we were growing up there were some things you said or did that helped me to become who I am today, so for that I give you a big thank you.

I can't leave out my grandparents Mr. Clarence and Mrs. Ethel L. Griffin, and Mr. Hebert and Mrs. Essie L. King. Although all are deceased I just thank God for them. They helped raise me as well; and it is also because of them that I am the person that I am today.

An acknowledgement goes out to my lovely wife the sweet Sandra G. King she has stuck by my side through thick and thin, up's and down's, through good times and bad times. She has been and still is a blessing to me and I thank God for her. If I had to do it all over again it would be with my sweet Sandra.

To my children Veronica, Dramon, Jemyrus, and granddaughters Katana, Malaysia, and Alaysia you are my driving force. You are what makes me want to set the example of being a real dad, father, grandfather and a true man. You see me for who and what I am, the real me. For with you there is no fake me, all of me must be real all of the time. I must lead by example. I can't expect to receive what I can't give. Thanks for allowing that two way street to stay busy all of the time.

I now take this opportunity to thank each and everyone that has or may think that they may have contributed something, good or bad in my life. You know, all things work together for good, for those that love God. Whatever you may have contributed in my life I thank you because now I am on top of my game and nothing can pull me down. It is through my good and bad experiences in life that I gain access to become stronger and better.

If there are no changes in my life then I will continue to be the same without improvement. God uses other people to move you off the road that you are traveling on (out of your comfort zone) and on to the side of the road sometime causing you to make another road; which will lead you to the road that He now wants you to travel.

Crying Through GOD's Eyes

Weather your intents were good or bad I thank you, because that little bump you gave me that knocked me off of the good road, and on to the side down through the thrones, snakes and bushes was only helping me to find the road with the path of golden opportunities. I would have not found it if it hadn't been for you.

I mean this in the most honest and God spoken way, I hope someone will soon bump you off the good road and on to the side so you too can find your path of golden opportunities.

To you the reader I thank you too. I know if you will read this book, through its entirety then some type of change will come into your life and my mission will be completed. Be blessed and have fun reading.

Last but not least I want to thank (Author) Ms. Desiree Lee who is the founder of http://dleeinspires.com/imready #no author left behind; solutions to get results.

Keith M. King

Contents

Introduction..
....ix

Chapter 1
Crying, Through GOD'S Eyes

*The explanation of how one must change his way of thinking.
*Operating from the Kingdom Prospective.
*Keys of the kingdom.
*Expansion of heaven to earth.

Chapter 2
What is Your Purpose?

*We all have a purpose.
*You too are full of **I AM**.
*Die empty.

*Becoming successful.

Chapter 3
Taking ownership

*Having a right to be successful and prosperous.
*Joint heirs with Jesus.
*The Ten Commandments.

Chapter 4
The Next Step

*Apply what you know to your life.
*Becoming a great leader.
*Supernatural abilities.

Chapter 5
No More Worries

*The covenant blessing.

*The kingdom of God is in you.
*Seek the kingdom of heaven.

Chapter 6
The Law of Faith

*Use expectation as a tool to work your faith.
*Impossible to please God without faith.
*Common wealth government.
*Sowing and reaping.

Chapter 7
The Holy Spirit & Gifts

*Separation from the Old Testament into the New Testament.
*The two parts of the Holy Spirit.
    *Supernatural powers.
    *Praying in the Holy Spirit.
    *The Father has to get permission.

Chapter 8
The Blood

Introduction

I would like to introduce the meaning of the title of this book. Many would probably say the title seems to say through the crying eyes of God, but that's not it at all. It is sort of an ambiguity. It depends on how one may view God as opposed to viewing him/herself, to get the real understanding of what is really being said. Have any of you ever thought that God is unfair to some people? There are some that are born into a wealthy family with no worries so you would think, right? Well as you may already know that is not always true. Well what about those that were born in poverty, but somehow made it to their successful goal in life. Then there are some that are born with physical and, or mental disabilities and nothing will stop them from reaching their full potential of success.

Out of the seven billion people that are on this planet, we all view success in different ways. For some it takes a lot to make them happy, and for others all they need is the basic needs in life to feel successful. My success level cannot be determined by you, nor can yours be determined by me. Given these two questions, are you happy, and if you had the power to change your situation to make yourself happy would you do so? Well my friend you do have the power to change your life if you want to.

That is the essence of this book, you will learn how to take what you have and turn it into what you want, through God's help. Let's get started and see just how it is done.

Chapter 1

Crying, Through GOD'S Eyes

God is and always will be there for each and every one of us through our everyday struggles. First we must change our way of thinking, for every born again believer the bible tells me that in Matthew 4: 17 Jesus said *"Repent: for the kingdom of heaven is at hand"*. This means change your way of thinking because Jesus has come to earth to give man the kingdom of God back.

The first man Adam had received the entire earth from God. He was given authority, and dominion over everything on earth except man. We must understand that God is real, Heaven is real and every word in the bible is true. Heaven is a Kingdom, or a government. It is more real than earth. Just because you can't see Heaven with your natural eye does not mean that it does not exist. God intends on us operating out of His governmental system to be prosperous in our everyday life. The earth is a copy of Heaven in the physical realm, one of the differences is earth is being destroyed daily, whereas Heaven is in its Holiest and purest forms of glory with no unrighteousness.

To operate out of the Kingdom one must believe hold fast to that belief and be able to see what he/she are believing for with the spiritual eye. When God made Adam, Adam was able to walk and talk with God every day without going into a religious ritual. Adam was given charge over the entire earth to subdue it and replenish it. This means that Adam had the ability to speak to things that were not as though they were. He was given the words of truth, also if you are a born again believer we have the same authority, if we can only believe.

Crying Through GOD's Eyes is about a born again believer living in lack, doubt, despair. It's about that person not understanding that God love them and has already fixed whatever problem that may occur. We tend to pray and ask God to do something for us that we have need of, but we don't realize that God has already did all that He is going to do. All things were finished before the foundation of the world was ever created. We have everything that we need, want and desire already waiting on us. One must be able to see with the spiritual eye and call those things that are not into existence.

Our Heavenly Father sees all things and has prepared all for us leaving us in a position that we should not cry, because we already have what we ask for. There are keys to the Kingdom. Here's an example to keep in mind, Matthew 16:19 *"And I will give unto thee the keys of the kingdom of heaven: and whatsoever thou shalt bind on earth shall be bound in heaven: and whatsoever thou shalt loose on earth shall be loosed in heaven".* Is this good? Need another one? Try this one Matthew 12:36-37 *"But I say unto you, That every idle word that men shall speak, they shall give account thereof in the day of judgment". "For by thy words thou shalt be justified, and by thy words thou shalt be condemned".*

This means speak blessings over yourself don't speak idle words that don't mean anyone any good. When words are spoken the atmosphere starts to make way for that which was spoken, good or bad. God made man in His likeness and image along with all that He made He saw everything that He had made, and behold, it was very good.

The only two perfect chapters in the bible are Genesis chapter one and two everything was very good according to God. This was before the fall of Adam and Eve during the encounter with the serpent in chapter three. Out of all the planets that God created He placed man on earth and gave earth to man to rule. God even placed man in a garden that grew every tree that is pleasant to the sight, and good for food.

There was also a river in the garden to water it. God put Adam into the Garden of Eden to dress it and to keep it and he could freely eat of all, except the tree of the knowledge of good and evil. God also made a woman, and brought her to Adam. They were both made to live forever with the command from God to be fruitful and multiply, and replenish the earth, and subdue it.

God's intent for man on earth was to expand Heaven down to earth. To say this in a different way is God had an idea the idea was through His thought process. Before God made anything He thought everything through from beginning to end. Your life, my life and how it is going to turn out is already known by our Heavenly Father. Nothing is a surprise to Him, therefore we don't have to beg or go into a religious ceremony to try to get God to do something for us. Everything is already done; we just have to know how to live from the Kingdom prospective to allow our blessings to manifest in our lives.

St. John 3:1-3 says *"In the beginning was the Word, and the Word was with God, and the Word was God"*. *"The same was in the beginning with God"*. *"All things were made by him; and without him was not anything made that was made"*. Word means (Logos) which means expressions of an idea. We are spiritual beings that possess a soul that live in a body. God could have so easily made us to worship Him without free will to want to do so. But He loves us so much that He gave us free will to choose, and make decisions on whatever we want to. This leads me to say the choices that we make have consequences either good or bad. It's our choices that tend to guide our lives.

Most choices are acquired through lack of knowledge and understanding. One can't do better if he/she doesn't know any better. It is important to position yourself in right teaching. The bible states that we must guard our eyes and ears, meaning we can't participate in any type of behavior that is not pleasing to God. Everything that we are searching for is already within us. Does a bird have to go to school to learn how to fly? Or does a fish have to be taught to swim? Both answers are no. If you have a seed in your hand what do you have? You have a forest that was produced from a tree that produced seeds that came from a seed that produced the tree.

God made all things to succeed He built into everything that He made laws to guarantee success. BIBLE – (basic instructions before leaving earth). God's book is filled with promises and laws, if we obey His laws and instructions we can't help but to succeed. Success is a result of decisions (good decisions) also failure is a result of decisions (bad decisions). Habakkuk 2:2-3 *"And the Lord answered me, and said, Write the visions, and make it plain upon tables, that he may run that readeth it"*. *"For the vision is yet for an appointed time, but at the end it shall speak, and not lie: though it tarry, wait for it; because it will surely come, it will not tarry"*.

You must write down what you want to do or become and move in that direction. Within each of us there is a burning desire to fulfill our childhood dreams; more or less this is what God has already planned for your life. Remember He has already finished your life, you must find a way to bring it into existence. We must remember that we are all born winners in God's presence; He created all of us to fulfill our destiny.

Success comes from knowing what the great Benjamin Franklin said, "If you fail to plan, you are planning to fail". Each and every one of us has a purpose in life, finding that purpose is the key to success. There are some questions that you must ask yourself to find your destiny. What is it that you think that you were born to do? What is the one thing that you really love to do? Do you have a childhood dream that still haunts you? What thing or things that you do that you could spend all day and everyday doing? What is it that you are good at doing that others really love for you to help them with?

These are questions that will help us move in the direction of our destiny. Success comes from within we all have it in us. Some of us find our destiny early in life while others may find theirs almost at the end of their life; nevertheless be grateful. There are some that will never find their true destiny.

To those that do find their way let it be known that sometimes things may go in the opposite direction that we might think they should go. But still hold on, sometimes God has to move us from one spot to another in order to bring into existence His plan.

Remember it's not about us sometimes He will bless others through us.

Though we may not see the direct blessing on us, we are still blessed through Him blessing others through us and He gets the Glory, not us. God's way is not our way. All things work together for good for those that love God. God is good all the time and all the time He is good! He is our creator the author and finisher of our faith and through Him we have our being. In Him we have all that we need and almost all that we want, if not all that we want.

It isn't hard to get off track of knowing that we have God on our side and He will handle all of our problems for us if we would only allow Him to do so. We must stay focused on what we cannot see to fix the problems that we can see. Remember that every situation and problem has already been worked out for us before we were even born. So don't worry when you worry, you show God that you don't trust Him and you have doubt. This will only hinder what He has fixed from the beginning.

Review Questions

Chapter 1

1. What was Jesus' purpose for coming to earth?
2. What is heaven?
3. What are some keys to the kingdom?
4. Why should man not speak idle words?
5. How many perfect chapters are in the bible?
6. What is God's intent for man on earth?
7. What does the word Logos mean?
8. What are the five questions to finding your destiny?

Chapter 2

What is your purpose?

Nothing is worse than living without a purpose in life. Believe it or not there are millions of people that walk around every day without a purpose, or a reason for existing. This is not God's plan for us to live idle with no purpose. He designed each of us with a destiny to become great in many different ways. We are all here to help each other in our short comings.

Here are some keys to help discover your Kingdom destiny that will surely get you on track. Do you know who you are? The first thing is to find out who you are. The real you is who God says that you are. For born again believers we are the sons and daughters of the true and living God. We are spiritual beings that possess a soul and live in a body.

Do you know where you are from? We all came from the thought process of God who is in Heaven. Do you know why you are here? We are here to live out God's idea of expanding His Kingdom to earth. The question lies what can I do? Well in Philippians 4:13 it reads *"I can do all things through Christ which strengtheneth me"*. This leads me to my final question where am I going? To me there are two answers. As long as I am in the flesh I shall be prosperous in all my ways and have great success as long as I live. And after this life I shall have eternal life with Christ Jesus.

I think by now you should be able to see that it is against God's will for anyone to not be happy or successful in this life being the fact that we are all born winners. It is the calling of each individual to find his/her purpose in life. When God says that He is "I

AM" I can see just what He means! For you too are full of I AM. Need examples, I AM blessed, I AM happy, I AM successful, I AM the son/daughter of the true and living God, I AM living with a renewed mind in the Kingdom of God. The list goes on and on.

Do you remember in chapter one when I said that you have the ability to speak things into existence? Well every time you say I AM, I AM starts looking for you through the atmosphere and it attach itself to you. And manifest God's blessings in your life. Also be careful not to use I AM in a negative way because that negativity will also start looking for you to attach itself into your live. Whatever positive process that you may have started with using I AM may be well on its way, but when the negative I AM comes out of your mouth it hinders the positive and slows down the process, thus making it take longer for the positive to come forth.

Your purpose in life should be to acknowledge God in all your ways and He will direct your path. Acknowledging God in all your ways is to live through the Kingdom prospective. This is the purpose of Jesus' death, burial and resurrection, to restore man back to the Father who is in Heaven. We are now restored back into the Kingdom of God able to walk and be directed by His precious Holy Ghost. You are chosen by God to do something important with your life. Do you think Our Father who is in Heaven is happy with us wishing, wanting, and crying about what we don't have when He gave us all that we need in abundance? The great T.D. Jakes stated that "success is accomplished when you know your purpose and accomplish things you were put on this earth to do".

The well- known Dr. Myles Munroe gave some good insight about how a person should "die empty". He states that the grave-yard is the richest place on earth, because it is full of dreams, unwritten books, songs, and pomes, full of unseen inventions and ideas. There are so many non-successes in the grave-yards throughout this world. We should all strive to release all that God has placed inside of us, tap into your hidden abilities and see how far you can go. Don't let the grave-yard rob you of your prosperity. Everything that exists first came from an idea that someone had in their mind. Even God had an idea when He said "let us make man in our image".

When the Holy Spirit speaks to you, you should listen and act upon what He says. That little still voice inside of you that tells you not to do something, or that you should do something. You should take heed to what He is saying that could be the difference between success and failure. If you renew (think in a different way) your mind like it says in Luke 12:31 *"But rather seek ye the kingdom of God; and all these things shall be added unto you"*. You will learn that all things are possible through Christ that gives you the ability to do all.

We must remember that we do not own ourselves; we belong to the Father and we have been bought with a price that has been paid for by our Lord and Savior Jesus Christ. There is nothing that we can do for ourselves except through the help of our Heavenly Father, therefore; if God doesn't do for us what is needed, then how else can we receive it? We depend on Him to breathe, to see, to walk, to live and everything else needed to allow us to exist. With this in mind we should now know that if we depend on the Father for our needs, then we must also depend on Him for our desires. The point is God wants each of us to be prosperous in all we do; He loves us that much.

Do you know what your purpose in life is? God has created everyone with a purpose or a reason for being here on earth. Don't think of yourself as just another person here to live for a while and then pass on without contributing anything to others that will be passed on for generations to come. We are all here to make a great impression in other people lives. Every great man or woman that has ever lived was just like you and I, the only difference is they saw their purpose to make a difference in society. Not only did they see that they could make a difference, they made the difference.

God has a principal; a fixed law that is established to guarantee the performance of a product. These are some principals that have to be applied to become successful in life. These six principals were given to me by Dr. Myles Munroe.
1. **Purpose** - a guiding vision- a glimpse of your reason for living. If you don't know your purposes then ask God to show you how to reach your destiny.
2. **Passion** – a desire that is stronger than death. Being willing to die for what you are going after.
3. **Planning** – write your plans down on paper and God will direct your plans.

4. **People** – know the right people to keep in your life. Don't let people talk you out of your dream.
5. **Persistence** – consistency, insist that you have what you are going after. You must be convinced that what you are going after is yours, and don't stop until you get it.
6. **Prayer** – commune with God. When you get tired or frustrated with being persistence, commune with God in prayer for strength.

God sees all, and as I stated before He has already fixed our lives before we were created; therefore following these principals is a guarantee to success because this law was set in place by God. Rest assure that there is no need to worry or be in doubt, that if you step out in faith that, God won't make it work for you. He wants us to be happy, to lean and depend on Him.

Have no worry our Father owns everything; don't be afraid to ask for big blessings, the bigger you ask, shows Him the bigger your faith is. That's what makes Him move in your favor. Be bold when you come to God's thrown of glory, this lets Him know that you trust and believe in His Holy word. Tell others about your purpose and plans; this will also help you to step into your destiny. It is never too late to discover your destiny, discover your true destiny today and see just how far God will lead you.

Our Father has placed inside all of us potential and the ability to create blessings for others. He did not intend on us just wasting our lives by not being productive with our gifts that He placed on the inside of us. It takes effort to move from one place to another, therefore in order to be productive we must stop being lazy and make our way to be successful. If there is something that you want and you want it bad enough, you will find a way to achieve that goal. This is true with all things; everything is achievable if we keep pressing toward that goal we will make it to the end of that task and start on another one.

This is the concept to keep in mind; I can do all things through Christ that gives me strength. Remember to stop saying idle words that won't help you or anyone else. Only say what you want and what is true that comes from the bible. When you say negative words they stop the process or slow down what you believe that God will do for you. He cares and wants all of us to be happy. God gets glory when we are successful through His provisions.

Review Questions
Chapter 2

1. Who does God say that you are?
2. What are the three parts of man?
3. Why should one die empty?
4. How do you renew your mind?
5. What are the six principles to become successful?

Chapter 3

Taking ownership

Psalms 115:16 says *"The heaven, even the heavens, are the Lord's: but the earth hath he given to the children of men"*. Now that Jesus has given us the earth back we rightfully have the authority and dominion that God gave to Adam back in our possession. This means that I have a right to be successful and prosperous in all of my ways, because I am a son of God. The word dominion has several meanings: ruler ship, lord ship, care taker ship, or ownership which means to have legal title to.

In Genesis 13: 14,15,& 17 *"And the Lord said unto Abram, after that Lot was separated from him, Lift up now thine eyes, and look from the place where thou art northward, and southward, and eastward, and westward:" "for all the land which thou seest, to thee will I give it, and to thy seed forever". "Arise; walk through the land in the length of it and in the breadth of it; for I will give it unto thee".* Until you can see it you are not entitled to receive it. Believing is seeing. This is seeing with your spiritual eyes, the clearer the picture the faster that which you believe will come. God has made us 100% joint heirs of all that our Lord and Savior Jesus Christ own. This puts us in a position of not having to cry, worry or complaint about anything that we may be lacking in our lives.

In the book of Hebrews 1:2 it says *"Hath in these last days spoken unto us by his Son, whom he hath appointed heir of all things, by whom also he made the worlds".* So by Jesus being made heir of all things you have lack because you are not receiving your inheritance that was promised to you from the Father. Faith is the title deed of what we believe. Hebrews 11: 1 says *"Now faith is the substance of things hoped for, the evidence of things not seen".*

Are you still not convinced? OK read this, Hebrews 11:6 *"But without faith it is impossible to please him: for he that cometh to God must believe that he is, and that he is a rewarder of them that diligently seek him".* In order to receive what is yours, you must come boldly before the thrown of God. By coming boldly is evidence that you know without a doubt who you are in the body of Christ. One word from God can change your whole life.

He wants us to fellowship with Him daily. The bible says that eyes have not seen neither have ears heard what God has in store for us. This doesn't only mean in the next life, but also in this life as well. With God there is no limit, He owns and have all.

There is nothing that He can't or won't do for us. We are His children and He loves us and has designed us to be blessed in all of our ways.

I like to prove what I say about God turn to Ephesians 1:3-4-5. *"Blessed be the God and Father of our Lord Jesus Christ, who hath blessed us in heavenly places in Christ"*: *"According as he hath chosen is in him before the foundation of the world, that we should be holy and without blame before him in love"*: *"Having predestinated us unto the adoption of children by Jesus Christ to himself, according to the good pleasure of his will"*. Also if you would like to you can read that entire chapter to get more clarity about these few verses.

The Kingdom mindset is what was restored back to us through Jesus Christ. We are not under the Law of the old Covenant (Ten Commandments) we are under Grace and Mercy; the Kingdom has been restored back to us.

This will prove my statement as well as it will also give you more understating to this book. Romans 4: 13-18. *"For the promise, that he should be the heir of the world, was not to Abraham, or to his seed, through the law, but through the righteousness of faith". "For if they which are of the law be heirs, faith is made void, and the promise made of none effect": "Because the law worketh wrath: for where no law is, there is no transgression". "Therefore it is of faith that it might be by grace; to the end the promise might be sure to all the seed; not to that only which is of the law, but to that also which is of the faith of Abraham; who is the father of us all". "As it is written, I have made thee a father of many nations. Before him whom he believed, even God, who quickeneth the dead, and calleth those things which be not as though they were". "Who against hope believed in hope, that he might become the father of many nations; according to that which was spoken, so shall thy seed be".*

There is one important factor that we must keep in mind. During the time of Moses the Ten Commandments were written and given to him by God to give to the children of Israel. These are God's chosen people. These commandments were only for the Jewish people. They were not for the Gentiles somehow every other race of people has included themselves in along with the Jewish race. See God already had a plan for everyone else. Like I said He finished everything before He began.

While I am on this subject let me try to explain it to you. God gave Abraham a promise that He would make him a father of many nations. God told him that He would bless him and his seed. For all that are not Jewish and are born again believers they fall under the covenant of Abraham's seed along with the Jewish decent born people that confess Christ as being their Lord and Savior.

I'll try to be brief as I can. In the book of Romans 4: 16 *"Therefore it is of faith, that it might be by grace; to the end the promise might be sure to all the seed; not to that only which is of the faith of Abraham; who is the father of us all".* He is the father of us that are born again believers in our Lord and Savior Jesus Christ. We are no longer under the law of the Commandments in Galatians 4: 13-14 it says *"Christ hath redeemed us from the curse of the law, being made a curse for us: for it is written, Cursed is every one that hangeth on a tree"*

"That the blessing of Abraham might come on the Gentiles through Jesus Christ; that we might receive the promise of the Spirit through faith".

Galatians 3: 7-9 reads like this *"Know ye therefore that they which are of faith, the same are the children of Abraham". "And the scripture, foreseeing that God would justify the heathen through faith, preached before the gospel unto Abraham, saying, In thee shall all nations be blessed". "So then they which be of faith are blessed with faithful Abraham".*

Abraham had faith that God would do what He said because he trusted God. Now don't get it wrong, Abraham only had faith he was not saved. Jesus had not yet been born; therefore Abraham only received the promise of the blessing of material things.

He did not have the blessing of the Holy Spirit yet. That would not come until after the death, burial and resurrection of Jesus and His return back to the Father.

If you can remember when the man on the right of Jesus on the cross asked if Jesus would remember him when He come into His Kingdom and Jesus told him today you will be with me in paradise. Well this paradise was an upper region, it was not in Heaven. It was a place set aside for the believers of Christ such as the profits of the Old Testament. This was a holding place for the Saints to wait until Jesus came and preached the word to them that were dead.

God is just; for all of the ones that died before Jesus came, they were under the Law of the Ten Commandments or living under the curse. The only person that ever lived that was able to keep the Law was Jesus. So this means that everyone else fell short and could not receive eternal life until they accept Jesus Christ as being their Lord and Savior.

Now on the other hand there were some that were in Hell. Jesus had to preach to the captives in Hell to give them a chance to repent of their sins. The Father has freely given every person a chance to believe or reject his Holy Word.

Every person of a certain age must be given a chance to hear the Good News of the Gospel of Jesus Christ before the end will come, and before they can be judged by the Father to have eternal life or be thrown into the lake of fire and brimstone. God is just and fair to all we are all His children and it is not His will that any shall be lost.

Let me show you why you don't want to be under the Law 1st Timothy 1: 9-10 says *"Knowing this, that the law is not made for a righteous man, but for the lawless and disobedient, for the ungodly and for sinners, for unholy and profane, for murderers of fathers and murderers of mothers, for manslayers". "For whoremongers, for them that defile themselves with mankind, for menstealers, for liars, for perjured persons, and if there be any other thing that is contrary to sound doctrine".*

You are free to go back and read this chapter for further understanding of what the bible is saying. Now let me show you why you would want to be the seed of Abraham Genesis 12:2-3 *"And I will make of thee a great nation, and I will bless thee, and make thy name great; and thou shalt be a blessing"; "and I will bless them that bless thee, and curse him that curseth thee; and in thee shall all families of the earth be blessed".*

Abraham was very rich with material things he had the blessing from God on his life. His wife was a very beautiful lady even in her old age in verse 14 it stated that when Abram was come into Egypt the Egyptians beheld the woman that she was very fair. God promised Abraham all of the land as far as he could see from North, South, East and West.

Genesis 13: 2 says *"And Abram was very rich in cattle, in silver, and gold".* In verse 5 and 6 it says *"And Lot also, which went with Abram, had flocks, and herds, and tents". "And the land was not able to bear them that they might dwell together; for their substance was great, so that they could not dwell together".*

In the book of Hebrews chapter seven it talks about Melchisedec the king of Salem being a priest of the most high God who met with Abraham and blessed him. It states that Melchisedec King of Salem which is King of peace without father, without mother descent, having neither beginning of days, nor end of life.

Now turn to the book of Genesis 14:18-19 *"And Melchizedek king of Salem brought forth bread and wine; and he was the priest of the most high God". "And he blessed him, and said Blessed be Abram of the most high God, possessor of heaven and earth".* As you can see this verse says that Abram was blessed by Melchizedek king of Salem and was called the possessor of Heaven and earth. God gave Abraham everything that He Himself owned.

Now if you would read Deuteronomy 28th chapter you will see just how blessed Abraham was and his seed. This blessing came not from the law of the Ten Commandments but from Grace and Mercy through the death burial and resurrection of our Lord and Savior Jesus Christ. God said that He will write the law on our heart which is being guided by the Holy Spirit.

See man didn't know that he was sinning until the Law (Ten Commandments); because he was never told by God that he was sinning. So God wrote His commandments down so man could see that what he was doing was not pleasing to God. God knew that man could not keep the commandments because if you break one of them, then you have failed in God's sight. God was trying to get them to a point of them knowing that they needed a savior. He wanted them to see that they couldn't save themselves they had to depend on Him for everything, but they still didn't get it. They thought that they were good enough to save their own souls.

During the time of Moses God did everything for His children because He loved them even though they were sinning and complaining. The Israelites asked God to stop doing for them through love and provide for them based upon their performance. The Father was providing everything that they needed food, light, heat, shade from the sun; everything they needed and wanted. They thought that they could please God through their own efforts. They still didn't know that they were sinning because God had not told them yet; He was providing all that they needed because of love. So God answered their request.

This is when God wrote the Ten Commandments. Knowing that they couldn't keep the written Laws (Ten Commandments), God still made a way for them because of love; He told them that they could make yearly blood sacrifices that He would honor because He knew that they would still sin. You may refer to the books of Joshua, Exodus and Genesis as references to this.

The Gentiles fall under Grace and Mercy through the final (blood) sacrifice of our Lord and Savior Jesus Christ. Now the Laws are written in our hearts and not on tables of stone. Once we have confessed Christ as being our Lord and Savior this is when the

Holy Ghost comes in our hearts and leads us the way God intends for us to live our lives. By saying the previous statement I must inform you of this. You as a born again believer that has confessed Christ as being your Lord and Savior must also remember that there is nothing that you can do to make God love you any more than He already does.

Therefore, your own efforts will not please God He doesn't want us to use our own efforts in life. He wants us to lean and trust in Him to provide for us. This is what the Kingdom of God is all about; depending on our Lord and Savior for everything. Just ask Him and He will provide all that we need and want. Then we will be able to boast only on Him and not on what we have done, because we can't do anything except through Christ.

Our Father is the King and we are the citizens of His Kingdom. The King takes care of His citizens of His Kingdom. He provides for them everything that they need because He rules and owns everything. The Father has the ability to manifest into existence anything that He wants, anywhere He wants. He has unlimited supernatural powers and abilities. He is GOD ALMIGHTY!

Review Questions

Chapter 3

1. What is it that Jesus gave back to man?
2. We are joint heirs to what?
3. Why are we no longer under the law of the old covenant?
4. What is the old covenant?
5. Who did God promise that he would make the father of many nations?

Chapter 4

The next step

The next big step is to take everything that you have learned and apply it to your everyday life. Don't get discouraged if things don't happen overnight, the key is in knowing, that you have started the process. The race is not given to the swift or to the strong, but to those that endure to the end. Just strive in faith one day at a time and you will reach your destination.

Now that you have learned a few things about how God's Kingdom operates, it is your responsibility to not only think of yourself. As you prosper teach others to become believers in God's word as well. Share the provisions of the Kingdom to others that the gospel of the Kingdom may go into all parts of the world. Our Heavenly Father is the master in giving, by us being created in His image enlightens me to know that I too must give, give, and give more. After all we can't beat God giving. The more we give, the more He will give back to us.

Giving does not always come in what some may consider being a painful way, of giving money, but it also comes in the most expressive form of giving thanks to our Heavenly Father. Let God know how grateful you are. Thank God for everything all day long, after all He is our great "**I AM**". When giving thanks it is important to worship God in spirit and in truth. Pray in the spirit as much as possible; connect your spirit with His spirit. It is also very important to meditate on the word. This allows you to eat the word, live the word, know the word, and be a doer of the word.

Always confess the word over yourself this will help increase your faith, thus making it possible for the word to manifest in your life. Be open to the Holy Spirit. Acknowledge Him by talking to Him every day. Not only should we talk to Him, but also listen to what He tells you, hear His voice. As you sow seed, and give to others give from the right motives. Have a willing heart and decide to walk in love towards your sisters and brothers in Christ.

Every great leader has to also be a great follower. By saying this I mean one must not be so high and mighty that he/she can't be told anything. Don't be the type of person that knows everything, have been everywhere, and have no room for improvement. This type of person in God's sight is very ungodly and selfish. Stay humble being true to God, others and to yourself as well. This allows the Father to reward you with even greater blessings.

Remember it is not about you it's about Jesus our Lord and Savior. The focus should be on trying to bring as many souls to Christ as you can. It's not about how blessed you are it's about fulfilling the will of God. Sometimes when you focus on doing all you can for others God will bring you up on another level. You will find yourself in a position that you never thought could be possible. Keep striving day after day to become the best that you can be, don't get complacent and satisfied where you are. Continue to try to move up to the next level striving to advance someone else along with you. Always try to bless as many as you can through the help of Christ Jesus.

If you comply with these steps one day you might find yourself not needing a job, or too busy to have a job. Your conforming to these steps may lead you into employing others to work for you, thus expanding the Kingdom of God in others' lives here on earth. When you get to this stage in your life you will be able to see that you are truly living in the Kingdom of God, under another form of government system, God's system. This has been His intent for all of His children all along.

No man has the right to boast about anything, God allows it to rain on the just as well as the unjust. Be thankful and continue to bless others through the blessings that you receive from God. Always remember what it says in Galatians 6:7 *"Be not deceived; God is not mocked: for whatsoever a man soweth, that shall he also reap"*.

It is time to start living from the supernatural abilities that God has place on the inside of you. Having the mindset that all things are possible and I can do all things through Christ who lives in me. I am a living witness that if you want something bad enough and you go after it you will achieve it in due season. Nevertheless don't be discouraged if you have pressed and pressed toward your desire but it seems like it just won't come to pass. Just keep holding on, sometimes you may be thinking too low for yourself, or thinking out of context with God, just keep the faith God will bring you through it.

He in fact may bless you with more than you were asking for at first. He can do that He is God "Alfa and Omega". God loves to challenge your faith, that's just how He operates. But trust me once He challenges your faith and He see that you will trust Him no matter what, and then will you be blessed with what you believe God for.

He is always in time for everything; we tend to think that if we don't get something when we want it that it will be too late. Have no fear our Heavenly Father knows all things; He knows when we are due our blessings from Him. Our yes maybe a disaster in our lives at that time, but His yes is always at the right time. All we have to do is hold on to our belief and trust in Him and everything will be alright.

I too must decide on my next step after I finish this book. I can't stop and sit in one place waiting on God to push me to the next level. He's not going to do that. The Holy Spirit will lead me to take the next step. He guides me in the direction that I need to go in and once I am in place it's up to me to listen to Him for guidance on what to do next.

We should never accomplish one dream and stop. Once we have finished one task we should start on the next, there is too much that God has put on the inside of us to ever stop. Remember to try to "Die Empty" by not hiding your gifts if God gave them to you bless others with them.

Review Questions

Chapter 4

1. At this point what is your next step?
2. How many different ways can you think of to give to others?
3. What does confessing the word over yourself do to help you?

Chapter 5

No More Worries

No more worries for you who are born again believers in the body of Christ. He has answered all of our needs, wants and desires forever. In the book of Deuteronomy 8:18 it states *"But thou shalt remember the Lord thy God: for it is he that giveth thee power to get wealth, that he may establish his covenant which he swear unto thy fathers, as it is this day"*. This deals with the covenant that God promised Abraham and his seed.

We as born again believers are under this covenant which is blessings and blessings. Now on the other hand, Deuteronomy 8: 19 states *"And it shall be, if thou do at all forget the Lord thy God, and walk after other gods, and serve them, and worship them, I testify against you this day that ye shall surely perish"*. This tells me that God is saying that He will give us all that we want and need, but if after we receive whatever things that we are asking from Him and decide to put those things before Him, or forget how we received our blessings, then we are not entitled to inherit eternal life.

I pray that you haven't missed the mark; my main focus is on living in the Kingdom of God here on earth. The word says in Matthew 4:17 *"From that time Jesus began to preach, and to say, Repent: for the kingdom of heaven is at hand"*. Jesus is saying change your way of thinking. The Kingdom of Heaven is a new way of thinking, a new government and new economy, renew your mind to new laws of the Kingdom of Heaven. Isaiah 9: 6-7 says it like this *"For unto us a child is born, unto us a son is given: and the government shall be upon his shoulder: and his name shall be called Wonderful, Counsellor, The mighty God. The everlasting Father, The Prince of Peace". "Of the increase of his government and peace there shall be no end, upon the throne of David, and upon his kingdom, to order it, and to establish it with judgment and with justice from henceforth even forever. The zeal of the Lord of host will perform this".*

I say to you all the old traditional way of thinking about the church has to be corrected. We must take back what Satan stole from us which is the Kingdom of Heaven. Jesus has given all things back to mankind. We were given supernatural powers through Christ. St. John 18: 36 *"Jesus answered, My kingdom is not of this world: if my kingdom were of this world, then would my servants fight, that I should not be delivered to the Jews: but now is my kingdom not from hence".* Do you want to know where the Kingdom of God is?

It is explained in the book of Luke 17: 20-21 *"And when he was demanded of the Pharisees, when the kingdom of God should come, he answered them and said, The kingdom of God cometh not with observation": " Neither shall they say, Lo here! or, lo there! for, behold, the kingdom of God is within you".* I say to you believers trust in God with all of your heart and you will enter into the Kingdom of God.

The Kingdom of God is in you; therefore we must trust and depend on Him for not some but all things. Sometimes we forget that it is our Heavenly Father who gives us strength to exist, without Him we would vanish. We were designed to serve God and God only He is our creator or manufacturer,

Therefore; we must stay humble to Him. When Jesus was tempted by Satan these were the words of Jesus to Satan in Matthew 4: 10 *"Then saith Jesus unto him, Get thee hence, Satan: for it is written, Thou shalt worship the Lord thy God, and him only shalt thou serve".* It is our Heavenly Father that provides for us all of our needs. There may be some of you that are in lack of many things, health, wealth, love, or even understanding. No matter what is missing in your life our Father is able to provide all to you in abundance by means of Kingdom life that He has prepared for us.

God has established laws that govern this earth and all that is in it. For everything there is a law on which it operates. The law of gravity for instance, if a book is dropped from your hand to your feet, or from the top of a building to the ground, the effects will still be the same. The book will fall down to the ground. This law will be effective every time it is applied. This is the law of gravity that was set in place by God. There is also a law of flight, if an airplane goes fast enough on the runway the wind speed will create the law of lift which cause the airplane to lift from the ground.

There is also a law of seed time's harvest. If you were to plant a seed of any kind, if planted in the right conditions, with the right sunlight, water and soil the seed will produce of its kind. These are laws that our Heavenly Father has put in place to govern all that He has created.

We as born again believers can also sow seed of any kind. There is a love seed, if you want to be loved you must show love to someone else. If you want to have friends, then you must show yourself friendly, and

The list goes on. Always remember whatsoever a man sow, that shall he also reap.

Take the money seed for instance, if you sow your tithes and offerings to God first and sow in good soil then God shall bless you as it says in Deuteronomy 28: 12-13 *"The Lord shall open unto thee his good treasure, the heaven to give the rain unto thy land in his season, and to bless all the work of thine hand: and thou shalt lend unto many nations, and thou shalt not borrow"*. *"And the Lord shall make thee the head, and not the tail; and thou shalt be above only, and thou shalt not be beneath; if that thou hearken unto the commandments of the Lord thy God, which I command thee this day, to observe and to do them"*. This is a law set in place by God Himself and He cannot lie.

God has so plainly said it in so many different ways that we can have our needs meet. He will bless us beyond our expectations if we only just do what He asks us to do. God sees all things, He has already made provisions for our every need, and everything is already fixed for us to prosper. It's left up to us to step into the blessings that are already there. My bible tells me that the Father already knows the things that I have need of and the things that I desire.

Therefore if I seek the Kingdom of Heaven first and minister to the saved as well as the unsaved and strive to be righteous in all of my ways then all things that the Father knows that I have need of He will grant them unto me. Needless to say, I try not to worry about life because I already know that my problems are already worked out.

I know that crying, whining and complaining won't do me any good, so why should I do this when it says in Matthew 7: 7 *"Ask, and it shall be given you: seek, and ye shall find; knock, and it shall be opened unto you".* And then Matthew 7: 8 says *"For every one that asketh receiveth: and he that seeketh findeth: and to him that knocketh it shall be opened".* This tells me that I should not worry about anything, that's living from the Kingdom prospective. If you take notice to the words Ask- Seek – Knock =ASK.

There are a lot of people that I talk to about living from this prospective, a lot of them hear what I say but it is hard to convince them to try to live in this manner. I always hear "yeah I hear you, but". There's usually always a "but". I try to tell them that these are not my words; they come straight from the bible. I can even show them the scriptures and let them read them for themselves but they still don't want to believe what they are reading. Faith cometh by hearing and by hearing the word of God.

If you are one of those that have purchased this book and you decide to spread the truth about the word to someone else and they sort of blow you off. Don't feel bad or give up on telling others keep right on spreading the word. After all they killed Jesus who is the living word, so you can expect to be not accepted by some. All you can do is plant the seed and pray that it catch root to spread abroad.

The biggest thing to remember is that you are not running the show anyway, so why not let God run it for you and you just sit back and enjoy His blessings. After all He is in control whether you reap the benefits or not.

Psalms 24: 12-14 says *"What man is he that feareth the Lord? Him shall he teach in the way that he shall choose". "His soul shall dwell at ease: and his seed shall inherit the earth". "The secret of the Lord is with them that fear him; and he will shew them his covenant".* Simply put if a man obeys the Lord which is to fear Him and He that can harm the soul. Then the Lord will lead that man through this life's journey with ease, though there may be times of troubles the Lord will see you through them. The Lord will also bless the children of that man that they too may walk in the blessings of the Lord, for this is the covenant that God made with Abraham. He will supply all of our needs if we will allow Him to do so, we are His children.

Even though God is our Heavenly Father and has already worked out everything for us before He created the Heavens and the earth; He will not step in, in times of trouble until we ask Him to do so. This is God's nature He is waiting on us with open arms. Although we were given the ability to decide and choose what we want in life we must first reach out to Him to allow God to manifest our needs into existence. To me this seems like a worry free life in a win-win situation. I don't know who wouldn't want to live in the Kingdom of God. Just remember if you are reading this book and you understand these methods, now you are obligated to tell others about the Kingdom of God, He will hold you accountable if you don't.

When you tell others this is what will happen to you. Coming from the 23 Psalms 6 verse says *"Surely goodness and mercy shall follow me all the days of my life: and I will dwell in the house of the Lord forever"*.

Review Questions
Chapter 5

1. Why should we as born again believers not have any worries?
2. From your perspective, what is my main focus in this book?
3. What is it that Satan stole from man?
4. Where is the kingdom of God?
5. What is it that God created to govern the earth?
6. What kind of seed can man sow?
7. Why should I not worry about life?
8. When will God work out our troubles for us?

Chapter 6

The Law of Faith

The book of Philemon 1: 22 says *"But withal prepare me also a lodging: for I trust that through your prayers I shall be given unto you"*. In this book Paul was in jail when he wrote this letter showing how we should use our faith. If you can grasp this concept you will see how we must use expectation as a tool to work our faith. Expectation is the key. Where two or more are assembled together, God is in the mist. Paul had already prayed and was praying when he wrote the letter to Philemon. But he explained to Philemon that through your prayers along with my prayers even though I don't know when I will be released from jail, however we will expect together and believe that God will answer soon, therefore have my room ready for me when

I get out of jail. This is how expectation will grant the power of faith.

Isaiah 30: 18 says it this way *"And therefore will the Lord wait, that he may be gracious unto you, and therefore will he be upon you: for the Lord is a God of judgment: blessed are all they that wait for him"*. This says that our Father in Heaven waits on us to trust and expect Him to do what He has said that He will do for us. The same measure of expectation that He has for us should be the same measure that we have for Him. For most of us God's measure of expectation is far greater than ours. Have faith in God He will do what He said. He will do it; He cannot lie.

Psalms 27: 14 *Wait on the Lord: be of good courage, and he shall strengthen thine heart: wait, I say, on the Lord"*. Isaiah 40:31 *"But they that wait upon the Lord shall renew their strength; they shall mount up with wings as eagles: they shall run, and not be weary: and they shall walk, and not faint"*. I give you these scriptures because they are God's words not my own. This is how you enter into the Kingdom. While we are waiting on the Lord we are not just being idle we are in the word and using our imagination in faith.

Imagining on how it will be once the thing that we are waiting on comes to pass. By doing this we exercise our faith and allow our faith to grow stronger while we wait on the Lord. It is like going to work, you work the entire pay period and at the end of that pay period you expect to get paid. This is to say that you were waiting in expectation.

It is impossible to please God without faith. This comes from Hebrews 11: 6 *"But without faith it is impossible to please him: for he that cometh to God must believe that he is, and that he is a rewarder of them that diligently seek him".* He wants us to trust on Him only. This is a seed that can be sown called the seed of faith, expectation, or trust. By doing this you are blessing the

Kingdom of God through your faith especially when you tell others through faith what you have already received before you even receive the blessing.

Call those things that be not as though they were, or being able to see with your spiritual eyes. Remember if you can see it you can receive it. We must believe in the word of God because it is the only word that is true.

If one does not believe in the word of God it is not good for him/her. In the book of Romans 14: 23 it states *"And he that doubteth is damned if he eat, because he eateth not of faith: for whatsoever is not of faith is sin"*. This is plainly put either you believe or you don't believe. So it can be said that whatever is done without faith is sin. Don't put your faith in the world's system thinking that your job provides for your needs through your pay check.

This is the concept of changing the way you think. Your job may only have one way of provision, but consider God He has thousands of ways to bring money and provisions into your life. God's Kingdom has a perpetual supply of whatever we need. God's Kingdom will never run out of anything.

Don't forget it is God that allows us to have physical, mental, and spiritual ability to perform the job in the first place. He gives us the knowledge, understanding, wisdom, and ability to do the job. Better yet God is the one that allowed us to be hired on the job in the first place. We can't do anything without Him.

He wants us to lean and depend on Him to provide all of our needs. We sing songs that relate to us leaning and trusting in Him but do we really mean what we sing about? Better yet do we even know what we are really saying? There are too many times when a real crisis hit home we tend to try to work out the situation on our own without even considering God for guidance to help us through. And quite often we still have to come to Him in prayer to fix what we have messed up. God is not our second or last choice; He wants to be our first and only choice in everything.

The Kingdom of God is considered as common wealth His government provides and takes care of all of its citizens. To enter into the Kingdom means that you no longer wonder about the five W's who, what, when, where and why. The Kingdom of God takes care of all of that. We were created with this intent in the beginning. Now that Christ has paid the price that allows us to enter back into the Kingdom we should enter into His gates with thanksgiving and praise His Holy name forever more.

There is also a law of sowing and reaping: this is to plant seed to harvest that which God has promised. Galatians 6: 7 states *"Be not deceived; God is not mocked: for whatsoever a man soweth, that shall he also reap".* The bible states that in order to reap blessings one must sow blessings therefore, if I sow the seed of money into good soil then I shall reap a harvest of money to provide blessings throughout the Kingdom of God.

In the book of St. Mark 4: 24 it states *"Take heed what ye hear: with what measure ye mete, it shall be measured to you: and unto you that hear shall more be given".* If one sows sparely he will reap sparely. But if one sows plentiful he will also reap plentiful. Nothing is ours; everything that we have has been given to us through our Heavenly Father. Don't be afraid that you will lose by giving, the more you give the more you will receive. Our Heavenly Father gave His all; He gave His "Only Begotten Son" JESUS.

Our Heavenly Father knows all, if a man sows one dollar and that is all that he has compared to a millionaire sowing one hundred dollars, who do you think that God is going to bless? The man that sows his all will reap favor from God quickly. God is not moved by tears, emotion, or even lack He is moved by the amount of faith that one has. I always have been a faith believing person because I know that it is God that causes me to have my being. I would parish without Him. We must find ways to build our faith, trust and delight our self in the Lord by keeping Him forever on your mind.

My sisters and brothers always remember this; never give up on life, yourself, or God. If we give up there is no chance to achieve our dream. Strive to excel in your present state. You can always do better than you are doing right now. We are born winners from God's prospective, He doesn't create losers. It is our choice to be who we are, if you don't like the present state that you are in, then change it. The only person that can stop you from achieving your goal is you. When you come to a stumbling block in your life; pray your way through it. The storm won't last always. Sow your seed of determination and you will reap restoration in the end.

Sow your seed with expectation of a specific harvest, don't be afraid to talk to the Father, let Him know that you are sowing a specific seed for a specific thing that you believe Him for. This lets Him know that you are bold in your faith of believing that He will supply that need. You have to commune constantly with the Holy Spirit. Listening to Him daily and following His instructions. This is known as living from the prospective of the Kingdom.

Audience please listen to me, there is nothing that you can do to make God do anything. He has done everything that ever needs to be done. We must hold to our faith to allow that which is done to manifest into existence by thanking the Father for doing it in the beginning; having it already waiting on us to receive it. Even though praying, fasting, reading scriptures, and singing are all good to do. None of these will make God move, He moves on faith and faith alone.

Whatever situation that occurs in life it is already fixed. Lack, sickness, broken heartiness, despair whatever, God has already fixed it for us if we only believe then give thanks for that which we are believing in through the Father; that it is done. This is living through the Kingdom prospective in earth. Just think of the Lord's Prayers when it says in Matthew 6:10 *"Thy kingdom come. Thy will be done in earth, as it is in heaven"*. God spoke everything into existence He also gave Adam the same Power and Authority, this is what our Lord and Savior Jesus Christ gave back to us through His death, burial and resurrection. We have a new way of thinking that does not involve us to do anything except ask, believe, give thanks and receive.

Review Questions
Chapter 6

1. Do you know what faith is?
2. How does expectation work in our favor through faith?
3. How do we know that God will do what he says?
4. How do we exercise our faith and allow it to grow stronger while we wait on the Lord?
5. How does God react to our faith?
6. What does it say in the book of Romans 14: 23 about faith?
7. The kingdom of God is considered as what?
8. Who is the only person that can stop you from achieving your goal?
9. How does one live though the kingdom perspective in earth?

Chapter 7

The Holy Spirit & Gifts

Please take note of this chapter it is very important that you understand how to allow the Holy Spirit to access your gifts for you. This promise comes under the new covenant, the separation from the Old Testaments into the New Testaments. The Holy Ghost brings understanding of the scriptures. He's a comforter, helper, intercessor, advocate, He brings strength and power. The Holy Ghost is a person He is not an, it. He has a personality; He is God's Spirit living in the inside of us that are believer in Christ Jesus.

I will start this chapter out from the book of Acts 1: 4-9*"And, being assembled together with them, commanded them that they should not depart from Jerusalem, but wait for the promise of the Father, which,* *saith he, ye have heard of me". "For John truly baptized with water; but ye shall be baptized with the Holy Ghost not many days hence". "When they therefore were come together, they asked of him, saying, Lord, wilt thou at this time restore again the kingdom to Israel"? "And he said unto them, It is not for you to know the times or the seasons, which the Father hath put in his own power".* **"But ye shall receive power, after that the Holy Ghost is come upon you:** *and ye shall be witnesses unto me both in Jerusalem, and in all Judaea, and in Samaria, and unto the uttermost part of the earth". "And when he had spoken these things, while they beheld, he was taken up; and a cloud received him out of their sight".*

Note there are two parts of the Holy Spirit. The first part is "Power" this is the Indwelling of the Holy Spirit inside of you. The second part is the "Holy Ghost is come upon you". This is the Infilling of the Holy Ghost, or the baptism of the Holy Ghost. These are two separate works of grace that the Father has given to us for a very important reason; we must learn how to utilize these precious gifts. St. John 14: 16-17 *"And I will pray the Father, and he shall give you another Comforter, that he may abide with you forever; even the Spirit of truth; whom the world cannot receive, because it seeth him not, neither knoweth him: but ye know him, for he dwelleth with you, and shall be in you".* This is the same promise that Jesus has also given to us. Luke 24: 49 *"And, behold, I send the promise of my Father upon you; but tarry ye in the city of Jerusalem, until ye be endued with power from on high".*

The book of Luke gives us a clear picture of how good the Father is to His children. Verse thirteen states *"If ye then, being evil, know how to give good gifts unto your children: how much more shall your heavenly Father give the Holy Spirit to them that ask him"?* The father is saying that He will give all that we ask for because He loves us that much and wants us to be happy. He is a wonderful God who supplies all of our needs and more.

Our Father is a right now God, He will move right now. We don't have to wait to receive the Holy Ghost. In fact we don't have to wait to receive anything that God has freely offered in His word. Acts 8: 27-39 *"And he arose and went: and, behold, a man of E-thi-o-pi-a, an eunuch of great authority under Can-da-ce-queen of E-thi-o-pi-ans, who had the charge of all her treasure, and had come to Jerusalem for to worship"*. *"Was returning, and sitting in his chariot read E-sai-as the prophet"*. *"Then the Spirit said unto Philip, Go near, and join thyself to this chariot"*. *"And Philip ran thither to him, and heard him read the prophet E-sai-as, and said, Understandest thou what thou readest"?* *"And he said, How can I, except some man should guide me"?* *"And he desired Philip that he would come up and sit with him"*. *"The place of the scripture which he read was this, He was led as a sheep to the slaughter; and like a lamb dumb before his shearer, so opened he not his mouth: in his humiliation his judgment was taken away: and who shall declare his generation"? "For his life is taken from the earth". "And the eunuch answered Philip, and said, I pray thee, of whom speaketh the prophet this? of himself, or of some other man"? "Then Philip opened his mouth, and began at the same scripture, and preached unto him Jesus". "And as they went on their way, they came unto a certain water: and the eunuch said. See, here is water; what doth hinder me to be baptized"? "And he commanded the chariot to stand still: and they went down both into the water, both Philip and the eunuch: and he baptized him". "And when they were come up out of the water; the Spirit of the Lord caught away Philip, that the eunuch saw him no more: and he went on his way rejoicing".*

This scripture tells me that if a person says that he/she wants to receive or be baptized, there shouldn't be any time wasted. It should be done right then and there. This is why we must change our way of thinking in the old traditional way of thinking. We should be thinking with the Kingdom mindset. This is why Jesus came to fulfill the law which is now written on our hearts and not on stone. The church is in us, not in a building. We assemble together in the building, but we are the church.

Acts 14: 7-11 says *"And there they preached the gospel, and there sat a certain man at Lys-tra, impotent in his feet, being a cripple from his mother's womb, who never had walked"*. *"The same heard Paul speak: who steadfastly beholding him, and perceiving that he had faith to be healed"*. *"Said with a loud voice, Stand upright on thy feet, and he leaped and walked"*. *"And when the people saw what Paul had done, they lifted up their voices, saying in the speech of Ly-ca-o-ni-a, the gods are come down to us in the likeness of men"*. The power of God still works the same today, if we only believe. This man believed and received, he was healed right away with no hesitation.

Here is another scripture to show you that you can have what you say right away. Acts 9: 17-18 *"And An-a-ni-as went his way, and* *entered into the house; and putting his hands on him said, Brother Saul, the Lord, even Jesus, that appeared unto thee in the way as thou camest, hath sent me, that thou mightiest receive thy sight, and be filled with the Holy Ghost". "And **immediately** there fell from his eyes as it had been scales: and he received sight forthwith, and arose, and was baptized".*

It is important that we understand that the Holy Spirit will allow us to see what others can't see. He helps us to understand the scriptures which will allow us to receive power and the ability to produce supernatural fruit. This is what God means when He says you will have peace that surpasses all understanding having the ability to operate from the supernatural. Sometimes you won't even understand how certain things came to pass. Stop looking at life from a natural state, for we are not natural beings. We are Spiritual beings that possess a soul and we live in a body, therefore don't be coronial minded. God wants us to think as Kings and Queens, sons and daughters of the Most High God.

Our Father has already finished everything all that we want and need is already waiting on us to ask for it. The problem is we don't know how to ask for what we want through our natural bodies. God told us that our way is not His way; our thoughts are not His thoughts. This is why we need the Holy Spirit to lead us into the truth. Do you remember that the bible states that in order to pray to God we must come to Him in Spirit and in Truth?

This is why we must be baptized in the Holy Spirit that we may receive utterance to communicate to the Father. When the Holy Spirit in you connects to Jesus who sits on the right hand of the Father, then Jesus becomes our intercessor to God the Father. When we utter words from our mouth this is a language that we are not familiar with, therefore we don't know what we are saying. This is praying in the Spirit, the Holy

Spirit speaks for us the answer to our need or want then the Father will release that which we are praying for.

The Father has to get permission from us to do anything in the earth, He gave the earth to us with dominion and authority, therefore He don't rule the earth we do and He has to have permission from us to do anything. It is the Father's will that everything is well in the earth but if we don't know the keys or the laws on how to operate in the earth then the Father can't do anything for us. By praying in the Spirit allows us to pray the will of the Father to Him from us which allows Him to grant us the prayer that we are praying.

I must prove this in the bible so go to 1st Corinthians 14: 2 *"For he that speaketh in an unknown tongue speaketh not unto men, but unto God: for no man understandeth him; howbeit in the spirit he speaketh mysteries"*. You can also read the rest of this chapter of the book of Corinthians to enlighten yourself about speaking in tongue. The Holy Spirit Himself cannot pray He has to pray through someone that has authority in the earth; even Jesus does not have the authority anymore because He is no longer flesh and blood. Only man has the authority to rule the earth. When we pray to God in the Spirit we speak mysteries. Mysteries are hidden sayings that are truths that are hidden from Satan so he doesn't know what you are praying.

This is what the book of Romans 8: 26-29 says *"Likewise the Spirit also helpeth our infirmities: for we know not what we should pray for as we ought: but the Spirit itself maketh intercession for us with groanings which cannot be uttered"*. *"And he that searcheth the heart knoweth what is the mind of the Spirit, because he maketh intercession for the saints according to the will of God"*. *"And we know that all things work together for good to them that love God, to them are the called according to his purpose"*. *"For whom he did foreknow, he also did predestinate to be conformed to the image of his Son, that he might be the firstborn among many brethren".*

To pray in the Holy Spirit is not hard, submit yourself to God mind, body and soul. Think on him with everything now start to thank Him from your inner being and let words just utter out of your mouth coming from your heart. You won't know what you are saying yourself but the Holy Spirit will know what He is saying to the Father through Jesus Christ. He will be telling the Father the answers to your troubles which allows the Father to move on your behave. The Father already knows what you need and want, but He can't move until you ask Him through the Holy Spirit. Try to pray in the Holy Spirit every day or as often as you can. Now you are living from the Kingdom prospective.

This is why it is so important to get this word out in the earth. Satan knows that his time is not long and he will do anything to stop you from being blessed with your inheritance.

Review Questions
Chapter 7

1. Where does the Holy Spirit reside?
2. What are the two parts of the Holy Spirit?
3. What question did the eunuch ask Philip?
4. Why does the Father have to get permission to move on our behave?

Chapter 8

The Blood

The blood is used for all issues that we may come across in our everyday life. It doesn't matter what form of bondage that you may be under. The blood is used because it is a supernatural force that will provide all of our needs. In times of need we can ask the Father through the precious blood of His Son Jesus Christ to see us through our times of despair.

The precious blood of Jesus is the key to peace; it brings about a peace that surpasses all understanding. There is healing in His blood along with hope, deliverance, abundant life, forgiveness and all that we need to be made whole. Our Father has made a way for all of us to be made whole no matter what we may be going through. We can plead the blood of Jesus over any problem in life, any situation that we have if we appropriate His blood we will be victorious.

Jesus was the blood sacrifice for our sins; His shaded blood covers all of our sins. Therefore, we have the right to be righteous, holy, sin free, sons and daughters of God. Jesus paid the price for us to receive the full blessings from the Father. Don't let Satan fool you; do you think that God would put His "Only Begotten Son" through all that He went through for nothing?

All that Jesus did was for the Kingdom of God. That man could inter back into the Kingdom and receive his dominion, authority, righteousness, and power back that which the Father had given to man from the beginning. We are God's children and He wants us to have what He has. Do you not know that we were made in the likeness and image of God? This means that when God looks at us He wants to see Himself. Needless to say, do you think that He wants to see Himself in lack, hunger, need, or anything else that is not His will? No, I'll answer that question for you.

I hope that you can grasp this concept; our Father gave us the entire earth and everything that exist in it to rule over. We were made to only speak into existence what we want with no work involved. Do you know how wonderful that is? That is supernatural power given to us because we are not natural beings having a Spiritual experience; we are Spiritual Beings having a natural experience.

The key is to only believe, and if we believe all things are possible. As we believe we will find out that we must thank God for what He has already done for us through His finished work. In the book of Genesis it states that on the Seventh day God rested from His labor. This means that He has finished all that He is going to do when it comes to answering our prayers. Remember He finished everything before He even started. Our lives are already completed from birth to death; we just have to step into our destiny to receive what God has already blessed us with.

Recap

This book was written for several reasons. First I want to say that I have explained in this book that everyone has a purpose or a reason for living. There is something inside all of us that is screaming to get out. If you would pay attention to what you have inside of you that wants to get out you will be great with your success. God may have placed more than just one purpose inside of us that we were intended to create.

There may be several purposes or intents from God for us to do. This book was also written to inspire those of you; that God does not intend for you to go to traditional church services Sunday after Sunday and leave the same way you came. There should be some type of change in your life. If you have been going to the same church year after year and you haven't grown in anyway then something is wrong.

Our Heavenly Father is a God of change, Although, He changes not; life changes all the time. The one thing that you can expect in life is change, nothing stays the same. Some changes are day from night, the season's changes; we change from childhood to adulthood. Things may change around us that may look bad, but trust me they are for your good. All things work together for good, for those that love God. He makes no mistakes and He has a plan for all of us. If we are led by the Holy Spirit then He will lead us through changes with grace.

Changes in life are created to help us grow through the experience. Some changes are meant to allow us to help someone else that may be going through a much worse situation than we are going through. Then on the other hand; there are changes that are set in place to lead us to our victory. For without the change we may not have been able to appreciate the blessing that we have received through the change.
God knows that we are creatures of habit; we expect life to treat us only with good

deeds that we expect to have every day all day long. Any unexpected change that may occur in our life tends to move us out of our comfort zone; therefore causing panic, doubt, fear, and other stressful thoughts that we should not allow to take over. This is why it is important to know the will of the Father through His Holy Word.

If you are not being feed the word of God then you have some choices that you can make. You can find a church that teaches on Kingdom life here in earth, or you can ask the Holy Spirit to lead you and teach you how to study the word for yourself. There are too many means of getting the word. It's like I said you are the only one that is holding yourself back. God has fixed it that we can become or do anything that we have a desire to if you just follow the guide lines of this book.

You are the only one that can hold yourself back, not God and certainly not Satan. Don't give Satan that much credit or power;

he can't do any more than you let him. If you have read this book all the way through then I know that you have learned something that will help you to change your mindset and move up into royalty thinking about yourself. God didn't create you to walk around with your head hanging down in despair. We are sons and daughters of the Most High God we are created in His image and likeness.

We have learned that we are joint heirs of the blessing that God gave Abraham through Christ Jesus. This gives me rights to have what I say because the earth was given to me as being a seed of Abraham. Therefore, I am not living in lack, I am rich, I am prosperous in all areas of life. I too am full of I am just like my Heavenly Father. Who is **I AM.** He is my Father, my creator, my manufacture we share the same DNA now that I have been born again.

Now that you have read this book you know that you too must go and tell others that are lost about Christ. Tell them about the Kingdom of Heaven and that they must change their mindset about this earth. We are living under another form of government which is God's Kingdom; tell them that He has expanded His kingdom from heaven down to earth. Tell them that we are to live in earth just as if we were in Heaven. We walk by faith and not by sight. Before the Father started creation there was nothing, He spoke everything into existence and He gave us the same ability to speak into existence what we want through faith.

This will lead you into the full blessings of God. It will put you in the position of not missing anything, not needing anything, and not wanting for anything. You will have the full blessings that the Father wants us to have just as He gave to Adam in the beginning.

We must know that Jesus has restored God's full blessings back to us through His death, burial and resurrection. Now we as born again believers are just as Adam was; we too can walk and talk with the Father through the Holy Ghost. Everywhere Adam went he expanded the garden throughout his walk, thus leaving him prosperous in all areas of life. Adam was able to speak just as God did and the atmosphere had to obey, because he had power, dominion and authority until he allowed Satan to steal it from him. But thank you Jesus!! He got it back from Satan and gave it back to us.

This same intent that God had for man and the earth from the beginning with Adam, is the same intent that He has for man and the earth now. For God is the same yesterday, today and forever.

This book was written with lots of insight about the Kingdom of God. Not only that but it also has a lot of biblical scriptures to try to get you the reader to understand just how much God loves us and the plan that He has for **all** of His children.

God Loves You!

About The Author

Keith M. King is the Author of (1) "Crying, Through GOD'S Eyes" (2) "The Power of my Words!" (3) "The Open Doors of Success" and (4) "The Open Doors of Success" Volume II.

Keith is a retired veteran of the armed forces with over twenty-five years of service, and he is also a veteran police officer with over twenty-five years of continued service. He is a graduate from Alcorn State University with a Bachelor Degree in Criminal Justice.

He is a columnist for two local newspapers, and one local magazine publisher. He has been provided numerous opportunities to conduct speaking engagements at different churches, schools, and other organizational functions around his surrounding area, about various chapters from his books.

Keith has received a certificate of honor from the United States Congressman; Honorable: Bennie G. Thompson and the House of Representatives in

Washington D.C. for his compassionate work ethics that he has provided for his country and local community. He has been featured in the Epitome Magazine out of Dallas, Texas, the Southern Writers Magazine that circulates throughout the southern region parts of the United States. Keith has also posted an article in the Alcorn State University's electronic newspaper that is generated to Alcorn's alumni world-wide. Keith is also proud to be a member of the worldwide group; Authors In Business #No Author LeftBehind featuring Author Desiree Lee.

Keith and his lovely wife Sandra have thirty-two years of marriage. They have three children Veronica, Dramon, and Jemyrus, three grandchildren, Katana, and the (twins) Maylasia, and Alaysia and two godchildren Courtney and Cobey. He is on the board of deacons at his church and loves to sing in the men, and the combined choir.

There is a great desire in his heart that everyone reach their full potential, one of his favorite quotes is: Success is placed within all of God's creation, this includes you...

Keith M. King

Keith lives in a small community called Cannonsburg, it is half way between Fayette, and Natchez, MS.

Look him up on his website: http://kmoskingdom1.wixsite.com/kmos, or log in on facebook at keithking59@yahoo.com

Crying Through GOD's Eyes

Keith M. King

www.ingramcontent.com/pod-product-compliance
Lightning Source LLC
Chambersburg PA
CBHW071707040426
42446CB00011B/1955